YOU TOO ARE *Psychic*
ARE
EVERYONE IS

THE *Real* WORLD *Angel* METHOD

Trisha DOLAN

A Psychic Medium and Angel Therapy Practitioner's
proven program that unlocks and expands
your psychic gifts.

PRAISES FOR *YOU TOO ARE PSYCHIC*

"Trisha Dolan is brilliant! In her book, You Too Are Psychic, she clearly maps out a fun and easy to follow journey for enlightened, adventurous everyday heroes to identify new territory in their unlimited possibilities in strengthening their psychic and spiritual gifts."

- Jasper Dayton, Mom and Business Owner

"This book is fabulous. Very easy to read and laid out in a step by step process. Trisha did a great job defining each of the gift we have and She also shares different modalities to strengthen these gifts such as mediation, yoga, pendulums and tarot cards. Personally I have grown so much from Trisha's teachings. I never used pendulums or tarot cards before.
Now I have access to gain the answers to my questions myself and have learned to trust my intuition."

- Heidi Lombardi, Mom and Social Worker

"Trisha Dolan is an amazing teacher that has changed my life forever. I've learned to look at life now as being on an amazing roller coaster ride. Trisha has taught me the tools to make life easier and more enjoyable. I now look for daily miracles, I have been blessed by Trisha, who in my heart is my guardian Angel walking this earth. This book is a must read!"

- Pam Haley, Retired Nurse

"This is an excellent book for aiding those who are awakening to their inner awareness. Remember to breathe slow and while reading!"

- DeWitt Lobrano

"You Too Are Psychic, is a down to earth, easy and enjoyable read. The book provides instructions needed to uncover and strengthen the psychic gifts we all have. Trisha has clearly communicated the steps needed for average folks to understand how to use gifts and abilities to live their best life. Trisha Dolan's "You Too Are Psychic" is a must have in my library and I look forward to seeing more from her."

- Abby Poole

"Is there a better way to learn how to become aware of everything you don't know? I do not believe there is. Trishia Dolan teaches techniques that answer every question you have ever wanted to know. Become everything you want to become. This book is a compilation of everything I learned in class with Trisha. The book is easy to read and understand. My life is nothing like it was a year ago. Now I understand how to create the life I really want. I want you to read this book to elevate your skills. These teachings can be applied to any part of your life. Become a better you."

– Dodi Jahns

"This book does not disappoint! Awaken your third eye!! A guide to understanding different types of psychic abilities (claire's) and how they apply to you. It includes so much easy to understand information on so many things, such as pendulums, tarot and more. I strongly recommend to everyone interested in their 'spiritual' part ....read Trisha Dolans book. I am now motivated to do more! Don't forget to join her wonderful classes and presentations. "

– Renee Longtin

"I am so glad that Trisha wrote her book. She is such a great resource and teacher. She has been a good friend as well and I know she has many. With this book she can touch many lives to help us help ourselves to remember. The pictures of her being so vibrant are stunning as I have known her for years , she is standing in her power in a good way as I say not in ego. I am so proud of her creating this book finally . Wooo who !!!!"

– Kasey

"I have learned and grown so much from working with Trisha. Everyone would benefit from reading this amazing book. It is an amazing resource with so many tips. Trisha has blessed us all by sharing her gifts and knowledge in this book."

– Deann Nevison

Publisher

You Too Are Psychic - Everyone Is

Copyright @2022 by Trisha Dolan Enterprises, LLC

Available on-line at:

www.YouTooArePsychic.com

Library of Congress Cataloging Data

You Too Are Psychic / Trisha Dolan

ISBN: 979-8-800-272604

Legal Disclaimer:
If you know or suspect you have a health problem, it is recommended you seek your medical or mental health professional's advice.

Any internet addresses, phone numbers, or company or product information printed in this book are offered as a resource and are not intended in any way to be or to imply an endorsement by the publisher.

Book design by BrandWorx Productions

ISBN: 9798800272604

Printed in the United States of America

Visit us online to access these free resources:

 Get connected with my community

Join my Free community, Real World Angel on Facebook and engage with enlightened souls that say yes to connecting with spirit.

 Connect with a community of people that are awakening to the art of connections and enlightenment. **facebook.com/groups/realworldangel**

 CALCULATE your sensitivities to Mercury Retrograde

How does Mercury Retrograde affect you? Take this quick calculation and find out. If you have experienced any of these events during the last Mercury Retrograde period, mark your score for each of the different events.

Find out how sensitive you are to Mercury Retrograde. **www.RealWorldAngel.com/sensitivities**

 DISCOVER Angel Abundance Currency™

Accelerate your abundance with this proven breakthrough method to increase financial prosperity:

 Join now and receive FREE Moon Cycle reminders that increase your prosperity. **AngelAbundanceCurrency.com**

 APPLY to be a member of my Medium MASTERMIND Mentorship

The MASTERMIND Mentorship program is an exclusive community of industry professionals, healers and thought leaders—exclusive to those who qualify and meet specific criteria.

 Apply to be our next member
www.RealWorldAngel.com/application

To my beautiful family
for being by my side.

and

My good friends
for helping me along the way

YOU TOO ARE Psychic
EVERYONE IS
THE *Real* WORLD *Angel* METHOD

Trisha DOLAN

A Psychic Medium and Angel Therapy Practitioner's
proven program that unlocks and expands
your psychic gifts.

CONTENTS

Letter to the Reader 17

Introduction 20

CHAPTER ONE - YOUR FOUR PSYCHIC GIFTS

Which Clair Are You? 26

Claircognizance 27

Clairaudience 27

Clairsentience 28

Clairvoyance 29

CHAPTER TWO - PROTECTION METHODS

Bubble Up 30

Suit of Armor 31

Programming a Crystal 32

Room Clearing Creating Protection 33

CHAPTER THREE - YOU HAVE A KNOWINGNESS

Developing your Claircognizance 38

CHAPTER FOUR -
LISTEN TO THE VOICE IN YOUR HEAD

Developing your Clairaudience 44

Clairaudient Practice Exercises 45

Meditation Practice 47

Physical Exercise 48

Strengthen the hearing connection 48

Yoga to Improve your clairaudience 49

CHAPTER FIVE - TRUST YOUR FEELINGS

Developing your Clairsentience 52

Clairsentient Practice Exercise 5 4

Pendulum 5 4

Channeling 5 5

Psychometry 6 0

CHAPTER SIX - BELIEVE WHAT YOU SEE

Developing Clairvoyance 64

Clairvoyance Practice Exercise 6 5

Exercises to develop ease into clairvoyant activity. 68

Knowingness Cards 71

Tarot and Oracle Cards 72

Seeing Auras 74

CHAPTER SEVEN - UNDERSTANDING

Native American Story 71

CHAPTER EIGHT -
GRATITUDE MANIFESTATION JOURNAL

The Way to Accelerate Your Desires into Reality.... 78

Acknowledgments 210

About the Author 213

Join the Journey 215

Letter to the Reader

LET'S FACE IT. We all wish we could wave a magic wand and receive the answers to everything, even me, the person who named her first book You Too Are Psychic.

Throughout my life, uncertainty has stopped me in my tracks. Trying new things, being in the unfamiliar, taking risks, getting fired, getting a divorce, saying yes, saying no, standing up for my beliefs, standing up for someone else, recovering from spinal meningitis, overcoming cancer, turning a corner but not knowing what's up ahead: it's all scary. Sometimes I don't know what is more terrifying: being vulnerable and putting my ideas out into the world, being an entrepreneur and responsible for my success, or being a grandma who almost fell and almost crushed her newborn grandbaby.

But uncertainty and failing at something isn't as bad as you think. On the contrary, it can be a good thing. We're spiritual beings having a human experience; after all, We need uncertainty to help us ask questions, stay safe, avoid disaster, and make a run for it when we need to. Uncertainty gives us a reason to gain more awareness. It wakes us up.

And here's the thing: uncertainty is not calling the shots. It's not in control. You are. You don't have to let it stop you. You don't have to let it stand in your way. Especially when it's preventing you from reaching your goals and achieving your dreams, it is possible to feel freaked out, overwhelmed with too much information, terrified, or paralyzed to do something and then find a way and the courage to do it anyway. Uncertainty can be overcome. You have the power to strengthen your intuition and take action.

Inside this book are the guidelines that I've established that help me see, hear, know, feel and move forward with confidence and clarity. As a woman, psychic, medium, entrepreneur, mother, grandmother, sister, everyday hero, and friend, I have seen uncertainty rear its ugly head in more ways than one. But, the upside of all this practice is that I've learned how to have uncertainty and still do what I have to do anyway. And I know you will, too. I am honored to be your guide throughout my book and share how life is more fun when the messages are clear.

Trisha

You Too Are Psychic!

Introduction

_____

"Everyone is psychic. Within us is a wonderful
energy that can be extended from inside,
outwardly to others, and
connecting us all."
-Trisha Dolan

Life is changing fast all around us, and people seek
inner and outer change in their lives. We hear that
"everything is energy" and "we are spiritual beings having
a human experience." It's all true. And still need to know
how to make these truths practical in our everyday lives.
We are all connected through this thread of energy that
can also be thought of as a master consciousness,
considered psychic energy. I'm honored to be your guide
to experiencing a higher awareness of oneself. I'm so
excited to be here to assist you in discovering your
Intuitive powers. Recognizing that we are all psychic is
exciting!

I started my spiritual journey over 60 years ago. My
mom told me that I was an easy child because she would
put me in my playpen, and I would chatter away,

entertaining and talking to myself. As I got older, I continued to speak to my "imaginary" friends (my mother called them). As my vocabulary became more proficient, I would ask my mother about the people I saw in the room, not truly understanding that I saw, heard, and talked to people who had passed away, people from other realms. My mom always thought I was a bit different, but she didn't discount my abilities or encourage them. We didn't discuss my unusual talents of seeing, feeling, and hearing things that she, nor many people around me, understood.

Being raised in a military family was an adventure. We relocated every three to four years, allowing me to make new friends throughout my childhood. In addition, mom would navigate us through a different route when traveling between relations, driving through almost all of the 50 states. These grand adventures created the restless spirit within me to travel and see the world and relocation often.

Our family consists of four children - two older sisters, Cathy and Jan, me next in line, and a younger brother, Mike. We all had very vivid imaginations. My mother believed that children should be seen, not heard, so it was crucial that we entertained ourselves and not in an argumentative way. Not only did we make up our games, rules, boards, and game pieces, we also dabbled with levitation, seances, and telekinetic sight. We had fun that included a pendulum, a book, cards, and a cardboard divider; this game was a Christmas gift. We would sit at the table, me on one side and a sibling on the other, usually Jan or Mike. Jan would look at a card with an image on it, think about the image, and I would say out loud which pattern it was (telegenic sight). We would think about the card and guess which one was selected. The cardboard divider was in front of the cards so that the other person could not peek at the picture. Jan was a good transmitter, and I a receiver. I got so good at receiving (and guessing) the images that we added colors to the pictures, so then I told the image and color. I believe that this game strengthened my Clairvoyance.

Many curious kids play the levitation game. I've told my story to other adults who mentioned they too played the game when they were young. Levitating our playmates was so exhilarating and even a bit scary. Jan and Mike were good at telling a story, gory sometimes because the person would die in the tale, and we would lift them. One person at the head telling the story, four people around the person being levitated; only two fingers of each hand are used to lift the playmate. Then the chant began by all parties playing, "light as a feather, stiff as a board." Then the person at the head said, "We can lift them, 1, 2, 3, lift." At Girl Scout camp, we lifted a girl and walked outside of our platform tent; she opened her eyes, screamed, and fell to the ground. No one was hurt, but we laughed for hours!

Our family also had an Ouija board. I do not like this game. Being a sensitive person, I can feel the energy of spirits, and often, this device is brought through angry people. When you are "dabbling" in the world of the dead, it can be dangerous without understanding; where there is light, there is darkness; when the portal is opened, both light and dark pass through. Playing with the Ouija board, we didn't understand any of this, and it isn't explained in the "game rules" that come with the board. We eventually threw our board away.

Growing up, our family attended many different churches; in whatever denomination the Base Chaplain was ordained, that would be the doctrine we studied. I liked attending church because it felt peaceful, love, and a sense of well-being. It's interesting that some 30 years later, my belief system of the doctrines taught me by those Chaplains and other Ministers did not match my soul's feelings and thoughts. I've always had faith in God, believed in unconditional love, believed in something beyond this earth life, but not all of the "hell and damnation" stuff.

In the late 70s & 80s, I read a LOT of self-help and motivational books. During the 90s, I started voraciously reading Metaphysical books; I just couldn't get enough information into me fast enough. There was a hunger in my soul. I knew that what I was being taught in school was not what I needed in life. The two worlds did not match the understanding and beliefs; I didn't have a "voice" or knowledge to explain my confusion.

Traditionally continuing my education was important because working in the Corporate world was critical for advancement. Therefore, in 1996 I graduated from the University of Phoenix with a double bachelor's (BS/BAM) bachelor's in Science in Business Administration and Management. It was intended to help me get a better-paying job to support my family.

Through all of the new studies and reading, I became certified in many different Metaphysical modalities: a Medical Intuitive, Palmist Reiki Master Teacher, La-Ho Chi Healing, Hypnotist, Tarot, Numerology, Gems & Crystals, and Reverend Status. These certifications gave me the confidence and skills to teach these classes in the Metaphysical Sciences I also started having a booth at Psychic Fairs while still working my Corporate job; A Purchasing agent by day and a Psychic, by night and weekends – for fifteen consecutive years.

In 2005 I retired from Corporate America to do my "psychic work" full time. In 2006 I became Certified as an Angel Therapy Practitioner (TM) by Dr. Doreen Virtue. I asked Spirit, "WHY Why am I taking this course? I've heard and seen dead people since birth." Spirit replied, "The paper certification is for others, not you."

My education in Metaphysics continued, and I received three Doctorates: 2007 Doctor of Divinity, 2011 Doctor of Philosophy in Religion & Doctor in Theology. In 2016, The State of Texas no longer accepted my previous Reverend papers, so I took classes and became (re) Ordained. I'm now an Ordained Minister through the First Spiritual Church of Austin, Texas. It is a passion of mine to officiate weddings, and custom write the ceremonies. Marrying both of my children to their spouses was heartwarming, honor and pleasure. Presently, continuing Leadership programs in personal development helps me to be a better teacher.The teacher, being a student, continually learning, is vital to me.

The understanding came that continuing education strengthens psychic development. As my development increased, so did my confidence. The proper understanding that psychic development is a GIFT, to be cherished, grateful for, and shared, became my mission.

The next stage of my psychic life came in teaching, public speaking, and touching lives, one soul at a time, sharing my passion, messages from other realms "Who am I here to serve, and how do I serve them?" became my mantra, my guiding force. Teaching others that they too are psychic became the message to deliver. Helping others to understand HOW they are psychic seemed like the logical process Clients have asked me for many years, "What book should I read to help develop my gifts?". There are so many amazing books written by great authors explaining different Metaphysical methods. Still, it's challenging to find a "How To Book" on developing the various gifts of Spirit in one place, so here it is.

Get started on the right path using your smart phone and hold your camera over the QR Code below. Set your intention with my exclusive intention setter tool that will allow you to harness your four psychic senses and achieve breakthroughs while you are on your journey with my book because you too are psychic, everyone is!

SET YOUR INTENTION

HOLD YOUR CAMERA OVER THE QR CODE. EASILY SET YOUR INTENTION

CHAPTER ONE

YOUR FOUR PSYCHIC GIFTS

Yes, you are psychic. However, different people have different ways of receiving answers from Spirit. To determine HOW answers come to you, it's best if we start with an understanding of the various methods, called modalities. As part of the developmental process, it helps to understand one's strengths. Each person has the gift of sight, hearing, feelings, and just a knowingness. These gifts have terms and definitions; I call them the Clair's:

Which Clair Are You?

Claircognizance (knowingness), **Clairaudience** (hearing), **Clairsentience** (feelings), or **Clairvoyance** (seeing)

The definitions below can aid you in understanding how you receive information from Spirit. Each chapter following will have some practices to assist you in developing a more vital acceptance of your gift. Like any muscle in the body, it becomes more robust and reliable if developed. An example of this theory would be chin-ups. If you try to do a pull-up, but your arm muscles are not developed or strong enough, you can not put your chin up on the bar. If, however, you start lifting weights and developing the upper body muscles, you can strengthen your body to do pull-ups. Developing your psychic "muscles" will help the answers to come to you faster and more readily and give you confidence in the dependability of your communication style.

Claircognizance (knowingness) "Clear Knowing." Males seem to utilize this gift frequently. Claircognizant people may not realize they naturally receive detailed and accurate information from angels, Source, Spirit, God (however you refer to the energy). Males (and some females) are taught as children not to have feelings or strong emotions, not to be sensitive, so they internally develop their intuition. Women are usually taught to be discreet, caring, and nurturing, allowing their intuition to grow to a different level of sensitivity than men.

A claircognizant knows, without knowing, they know. Consequently, you may doubt the validity of the knowledge. Most people recognize this as a "gut feeling." I like to call it "data dumping from heaven." Then, the information (facts) appear, what may seem like out of "thin air."

Clairaudience (hearing) "Clear Hearing." A form of channeling Usually, Clairaudience is defined as messages in thought-form or voices from another realm. Angels are love.

They will never guide you to do anything harmful to you or your family. Some people hear their voice inside their head. Another sign of Clairaudience is hearing sound or feeling the vibration
of voices in your physical space. The voice may come from within your body, within your mind, or sound as if it's outside your head.

You know that guidance comes from angels when it is loving, focused, consistent, and not harmful to you or your family. *Hearing the sound or feeling the vibration of voices and * Hearing/feeling vibrations or energetic movement in your physical space.

Clairsentience (feelings) "Clear feelings" Also known as psychometry, is the ability to touch or hold an object, stand in a specific place, or feel a person's body and sense the energy encircling that person, place, or thing. We are energy; everything is energy. Therefore, when you feel the energy in a physical form, it is known as empathic or highly sensitive. Clairsentient Medium will experience or translate all energies receiving divine guidance through bodily sensations.

Clairsentients receive through sense of smell, taste and touch. You know the beloved deceased grandmother is near when you smell her perfume or favorite flower fragrance. An angel may shower your room with the aroma of orange blossoms to tell you of an impending wedding.

The primary way of translating these sensations is intuitive, gut feelings, and hunches. According to angelic

guidance, much of this style comes from the stomach region, and the stomach flutters,
relaxes, and tightens. Clairsentients get messages through their hearts and love emotions. For example, if the thought of doing something swells in their chest with warm feelings of joy, this is a directive from Spirit and the angels.

Clairvoyance (seeing) "Clear Vision" Literally "clear sight." Clairvoyance is often used to encompass phenomena such as telepathy, second sight, prophetic visions, and dreams. Our mind thinks in pictures. The images may appear in full color or simply black and white. Clairvoyance captures the images and interprets these concepts into an insight,
creating meaning or message from Spirit.

I utilize ALL of the Clairs but most frequently use clairvoyant and clairaudient. Understanding which area is your most vital gift will allow you to utilize your psychic skills. The following chapters have more explanations and techniques about the methods of communication and how to develop them. You, too, may acquire all of them to be dependable.

WHICH CLAIR ARE YOU?

HOLD YOUR CAMERA OVER THE QR CODE. EASILY IDENTIFY WHICH CLAIR YOU ARE.

CHAPTER TWO

PROTECTION METHODS

Defining which modality is your most vital gift then developing that gift will increase your confidence. Next, you must learn to protect yourself. When a portal is open, both darkness and light are present. Working in the light is my recommendation, it's more comfortable. Therefore, shielding yourself from the dark energy is essential and done through rituals. You will develop your technique, the one you resonate with, and it's important to do the routine every time you are working on developing your gifts or doing sessions for yourself or others.

Protection Methods:
Bubble Up

This process is by far my favorite. Do you remember the movie "The Wizard of Oz"? Every time Glenda, the Good Witch, entered the scene, she floated in a bubble. When asked, "Why a bubble?" she responded, "Well, to protect me from my wicked witch sisters!"

Creating a bubble of protection around you energetically houses your energy and protects you from darkness penetrating your shield.

You take three deep breaths. Next, open your mouth, visualize pulling silver color up from your feet, between your legs, through your Chakra centers (middle of your body), and continue pulling the silver light up and out the top of your head. Imagine you have an umbrella opened over your head. As you exhale with an open mouth, visualize the silver light coming out of the top of your head. As the light shoots up and over the umbrella, imagine it sprinkling like rain (off the umbrella) and around you, creating a bubble around your entire body. Like Glenda, surrounded by a beautiful, iridescent bubble of protection, you now have a beautiful silver bubble around you.

Sometimes I choose the color pink to create my Bubble, representing unconditional love. When I would send my children off to school each morning, I would yell, "Bubble up!" I often put bubbles around them, even (still) as adults and my grandchildren, sending them protecting energy.

Suit of Armor
This protection method is a great visual for children. In the 16th century in Europe, the suits of armor were created for jostling. The helmet, gloves, full-body, and feet were fully covered to protect the body from injury. They were usually shiny metal reflective. Imagine yourself fully shielded, close the face mask, armored up against any harm. Fun protection method.

Programming a crystal

Some readers and healers like to use crystals for protection or other uses during their sessions. It draws off negative energy of all kinds. Quartz crystal has a very high frequency. It's also a transmitter. It absorbs, stores, releases, and regulates energy. Quartz was utilized to develop transistor radios. Quartz crystals will amplify energy and thought as well as balance and revitalize the physical, mental, emotional, and spiritual planes. It can also act as a deep soul cleanser, connecting the physical dimension with the mind. It can aid in concentration and even unlock memories. Quartz enhances psychic abilities.

When choosing a crystal to work with, go shopping. It's more fun in person than ordering from the internet. The stone will "call to you." I know that that sounds weird, but it's true. We are energy; the crystals are energy. When you touch a stone with the same or similar frequency, you will feel something with an electrical charge, joy, a flutter in your stomach, or even the knowledge that "this is the crystal right for me!"

After selecting your crystal, it should be cleaned. Some people like to use salt; I wash my stones with soap and water. When running the gem under the water, imagine white light filling the inside of the crystal. After it has been washed, it should be programmed with your energy. You will tell the crystal its function mentally or out loud Functions may include, but are not limited to: protection, channeling other realms, healing, clearing a deck of cards (Tarot or Oracles).

The next step in programming your crystal is to hold it up to your heart Breath deeply through your nose and exhale through your mouth. Visualize the white light in the crystal during the cleaning process, flowing from the quartz to your heart. Thank the crystal for being of service and coming into your life, like a respect prayer. Now, the stone is ready to assist you.

Room Clearing Creating Protection

Our homes or work areas tend to gather energy and can become dense or stale Our energy fields, also known as auras, can collect the energies of others, causing us to feel sluggish or even depressed. Clearing our bodies, auras, and areas around us can release the lower energy frequency, also known as negative energy. Different cultures use several items to clear a room (& body) and create a space protected from negative energies.

- **Smudging – White Sage**
  Sage is used in many cultures and has been utilized for generations by North American natives as a "smudging tradition." When feeling negative energy, tension, fatigue, physical or psychological stress, smudging can clear the energy, raise your frequency, and assist you in feeling better. Grounding, centering, regaining your balance will ease and create a comfortable environment. Clearing your space regularly by smudging is essential. Also, using sage creates a protective barrier.

- **Palo Santo Wood** – This tree grew on the coast of South America and was introduced as a ceremonial product to clear energies and for grounding. The Spanish state that this wood is related to frankincense, myrrh, and copal.

It is from the pine & citrus family, so its aroma is a mixture of pine, mint, and lemon. Sage has a strong scent, so many prefer burning the Pals Santo wood instead. The properties of this wood are grounding clearing negative energy; utilized during meditation can raise one's vibration and, therefore, allows a tighter connection to Spirit. It is also burned to keep away mosquitoes and other flying insects.

- **Nag Champa - Incense**
Utilizing incense of any scent can activate specific responses. Essential oils have been documented to carry properties of mental and physical reactions energy around your living spaces. It is also a pleasant scent to use as a protective barrier.

Comparable to sage smoke and diffused essential oils, incense is known for purifying and cleansing. Unfortunately, incense may not be the best solution if you want to block psychic attacks in public (due to the fire regulations). Still, it is a great tool to use when gathering with others and cleansing away negative and stale energy around your living spaces. It is also a pleasant scent to use as a protective barrier.

- **Create a protection barrier.**
To begin smudging yourself with the product you choose, light the smudge stick and direct the smoke

around your body. Start at your head and sweep down and away, flicking and motioning the negative energy to the floor. This practice is called aura brushing Guide and sweep the smoke down around your head, arms, chest, and legs. I recommend that you ask for help from a friend to sweep the sage smoke across your back – again being mindful to sweep the smoke down to the ground where mother earth can absorb and heal the energy. Also, you can put the sage in a sage-burning bowl that is metal or burn-proof. Allow the smoke to become thick and heavy. Position yourself next to the bowl and perform the aura brushing technique described above. Turn around clockwise to ensure the smoke encompasses all parts of your energy.

Create a protection barrier in a room.
The product is lit, then starting at the doorway, moves in a counter-clockwise direction. The smoke should be flowing. Negativity can snuff out the smoke, causing you to re-light the product to create smoke again. While moving through the room, chant, "only light and love can be in this space, now and always." When passing by a window, move the sage in a crisscross method (like shoelaces on shoes), sealing off the window. Some people prefer to open the closet doors and smudge there too. The room should be processed three times around. Upon the third time, returning to the doorway, exit the room, crisscrossing the entrance from outside the room.

Creating a protection method before starting psychic development is recommended. It would be unfortunate to be bombarded by negative emotions, feelings, pressure, or even receive a "psychic attack." Avoidance is best created by shielding yourself. Find a process of protection that suits you best, practice it, have fun with it, and make it a ritual of standard habit.

"**Life is easier**
and **more fun**
when the
Messages are
Clear"

Trisha

CHAPTER THREE

YOU HAVE A KNOWINGNESS

Now that you understand energy more and have a method used (to use) in protection let's explore how you receive communication from Spirit/Source/God/Angels. Recognizing your most vital way of connecting and receiving messages can be comforting. The first Clair we will be reviewing is Claircognizance and describing methods of developing reliability in this area.

Developing your Claircognizance (clear knowingness)

A claircognizant knows what they know, without knowing where they know it. Consequently, you may doubt the validity of the knowledge I often hear cognizant clients say, "I don't know where I read that or what show I might have seen, but...." The information comes from the cosmic mastermind/consciousness/Spirit/Source/Angels/God, whatever you feel comfortable calling it. There is vast energy of consciousness of people in the world, people who have lived before, and even future lives, floating around, that can be "tapped" into.

Being gifted with Claircognizance may feel less "sexy" of the gifts - Not a true statement. It's simpler. The emotions of a cognizant tend to be in a less heightened state, which keeps the internal beliefs and anxiousness out of the way. The ability to "call upon" the required information isn't usually as strong until an activation process is developed. It is almost like a flash of brilliance occurs to you.

Claircognizant Practice Exercise
Remember to use your protection method before starting the exercise

- Sit comfortably, Freeing your hands and lap of any objects.
- Breathe through your nose, expanding your lungs and out through your opened mouth, releasing the air. Breathe deeply in this manner three times and relax.
- Thump your thymus (center of chest right above the heart-sternum) and say, "Balance."
- Touch your face lightly, under each eye, the center point, with the index finger of each hand (under the right eye, right index finger; left, left index finger).
- Close your eyes
- You may choose to ask a question
- Say the word "Receive."
- Imagine a swirling ball of energy out in front of you. It's

large. It can be as vast in your mind as outer space or smaller, the size of a basketball.

- See the energy move into streams of light and color. As you observe it, see the streams separate.
- Imagine one of the streams coming toward you. See it move faster, slower, brighter Whatever you observe is perfect.
- Now imagine this beam flowing into your forehead or top of your head.
- Breath it into your consciousness.
- Let knowledge be transferred to you.
- If you asked a question, allow the answer to be given. You may hear, feel, see or know the answer.
- Don't judge; just let it be. It is not your job to do any-thing right now. Observe.
- If you did not ask a question, receive what the Uni-verse would like you to know.
- Release your fingers.
- Breathe deeply, bringing your awareness back into the room.
- Wiggle your hands, feet, and open your eyes.
- Journaling your experience is recommended. If nothing happened, write that down. If you asked a question, write that down, answered or not. It's possible to receive the realization hours or days later of what was received by your mind.
- When you get inspiration to take some action - do it. You may do this process as often as you like. Something new may come up for you each time you do this exercise.

When I was in college, balancing so many things in my life was overwhelming at times. I slept with my textbooks under my pillow. Before falling asleep, I would tell Spirit that I was open and receptive to receiving my book's information. I only opened and studied the information in physics and accounting classes. The rest of the courses were completed through lectures, taking notes, and osmosis of sleeping with the material under my pillow. The knowledge is already "out there" in the vast consciousness of the Universe. There are Masters in the arts, music, science, etc., that have explored, created, designed, lived extraordinary lives. This knowledge can be researched on a computer or tapped into through our receptive minds.

Developing your Claircognizance might activate other gifts too. Remember, during your exercise, you may feel, see, hear information, which are the different modalities. Nothing is to be forced. There is no pressure on yourself in doing it "right" or "wrong" as there is no such thing. However you do, it is how you are receiving your information.

LISTEN HERE

HOLD YOUR CAMERA OVER THE QR CODE. GET ACCESS TO MY MEDITATION THAT HELPS YOU ACTIVATE YOUR CLAIRCOGNIZANCE GIFT.

CHAPTER FOUR

LISTEN TO THE VOICE IN YOUR HEAD

Another gift worth reviewing is Clairaudience. This is not as common of a gift for most people to recognize. Society has so many "taboos" on "hearing voices" that I believe it's ignored more than not available as a talent.

Developing your Clairaudience (clear hearing)

Clairaudient is a vital ability because I've heard "voices" at an early age. Having had chronic ear infections, tonsillitis, tonsils removed at the age of five created a sensitivity to noise sound. I'm not sure if the ear problems started the Clairaudience or if because I was clairaudient I had ear problems. My eardrums ruptured several times due to infections and reaction to medication too. In 1982, I had a tumor behind my right eardrum removed. The doctor told me that I lost 45% of my hearing in that ear. I have constant ringing in my ears (tinnitus), which I lovingly refer to as "white noise." What I find interesting is Louise Hay's explanation of ear problems "what don't you want to hear?" (Maybe the loud noises of siblings and parents arguing?). Having the gift of clairaudient has become such an innate part of my being, like breathing, that I would not want to know life without it.

It is unnecessary for you to have years of ear problems to be clairaudient, but most people complain about the high pitch squealing tones they experience. I believe the tones are a frequency squeal. As mentioned before, we are energy. Spirit is energy. The frequencies of the two energies are not necessarily matched. Sometimes, as we become more aware, the heightened awareness needs a vibration adjustment, like a radio dial that has to be touched, turned to get the strongest signal, and make the station clear.

If you think about the voice of an excited child, the happier, more excited it becomes, the higher the pitch the voice creates. Then as the child giggles and squeals with more excitement, the sound almost transforms into a high-pitched buzzing noise. So when communicating with the angelic realm, they get so excited that they are being heard, that their voices come in like that tiny, eager child, a high squealing sound. This tone can then cause a "ringing in the ears." You simply request the voices to slow down and lower their pitch. If you went to a doctor specialist in the Ear, Nose, and Throat, you might be diagnosed with tinnitus. There are treatments for the ringing in the ear, but they might stop your clairaudient gift.

Then as the frequency adjustment is made, you will hear a voice come through. I've been told that many clairaudient people hear their voice inside their heads. I hear the person's voice that I'm talking with during Channeling (i.e., if it's an Italian grandmother, I hear her accent, tone, and tempo). When I'm communicating with someone from another realm that speaks a language other than English, I have the assistance of a "translator angel" to hear the message in English.

When you are fine-tuning your gift of clear hearing, the message may only be a word. As you become more skilled in communication with Spirit, realize that they can talk rather quickly. You may request them to slow down and be more precise in their communication. I have had circumstances where the person in Spirit has a moving mouth, but I can not hear their words (clairvoyant-seeing). That usually represents a recent death. They do not know how to communicate yet, and their frequency needs to be adjusted. Another relative that has been deceased longer usually assists with that energy adjustment. I speak rather quickly when in session, channeling to keep up with the rapid transmissions.

Some people that have had a head injury, concussion, or ear problems, have adjusted their internal communication styles. The brain plays a significant role in processing sound. Research has also shown a correlation between hearing loss and other mental conditions; this could result from the brain becoming damaged, atrophy, where the brain cells shrink, or the connectivity is damaged. Exercising the brain can assist the hearing process and even the psychic connection of hearing voices.

Hearing the sound, feeling the vibration, or energetic movement in your physical space are all concepts of Clairaudience. It's crucial to understand the idea of negative and positive energy in this modality. They know that guidance comes from Angels/Spirit/Source/God when it is loving, consistent, focused, and not hurtful to you or the people closely connected to you. If a voice wants you to hurt yourself or someone else, do NOT listen as it's not of the light. Tell it to go away and put protection around yourself.

Clairaudient Practice Exercise

Remember to use your protection method before starting the exercise.

Meditation Practice

The answers lie within you. Being still, quiet, and respectful allows you to be in a place to receive guidance Meditation is a process similar to prayer. This process will enable you to obtain information. Why not make the connection more substantial and reliable if you already hear voices?

One way to meditate is out in nature. Sitting in the forest, beach, meadow, or just in a park allows you to connect with creation, Mother Earth, Source.

- Deeply breath in through your nose, out through your open mouth. Just as creating protection practice of breathing, relax. Slowly taking deep breaths help blood circulation and increases oxygen in your body.
- Focus on your breathing, but allow the various sounds around you to come into your awareness.
- Locate where the sound is coming from. This assists your mind-hearing connection to increase.

- This exercise will also allow greater focus on receiving information in a noisy environment.
- Your meditation may last 5-30 minutes.
- Take three deep breaths, allowing you to become aware of your body; wiggle your hands and feet, open your eyes, and be present in your surroundings.

Physical Exercise

Exercising every day, going out for a walk, jogging, doing yoga, water aerobics, even just gardening or doing housework, is excellent for increasing blood circulation. When you are "in-flow" with stimulating energy, you are tuned in to your body; therefore, you are one with Spirit Exercise can be a type of meditation practice for some people, because they find the "zone," their mind and bodies react with the same chemicals that are transmitted during introspection.

Strengthen the hearing connection

Doing fun exercises to get the blood flowing stimulating electrons to fire in the brain can prevent atrophy. That would mean that playing mind games might improve hearing. It has been my experience that these types of mentally stimulating games have increased psychic abilities. Maybe it's guessing the answers?

Some games to strengthen the intuitive connection:

Finding solutions to a variety of puzzles like crossword puzzles, word searches, and Sudoku helps the logical mind by connecting the visual and cognitive regions of the brain. In addition, playing bingo and card games, such as hearts, canasta, euchre, and poker, help amplify the thoughts of what will be seen next and hear in your mind the cards to hold or play next strengthen the intuitive connection.

Yoga to Improve your clairaudience

Yoga is popular and practiced for its range of health advantages. For example, there are yoga exercises that help you with your hearing. The main goal of these yoga exercises is to improve circulation in your ear and your brain. Since boosting circulation helps improve nerve functions and removes waste and toxins, the hearing has improved.

Yoga poses that help with circulation

- Tree pose
- Lotus pose
- Cobra pose
- Triangle pose

The following is an incident where I received a clairaudient message:

One day, my sister Jan and I celebrated a holiday together, and we decided to make one of our mom's unique dishes. Mom believed that making the frozen fruit salad recipe too often would ruin the idea of being unique, exceptional, and unforgettable. She thought it was a dish for holiday celebrations only. We did not have some ingredients to make this dish, so we went to the market. We smelled cigarettes upon arriving at the car with our groceries (Clairsentient). Our mother passed from the effects of lung cancer, being a 3-pack a day smoker for many years, and since her passing, she decided that was the fragrance she would use to let us know she was around. I knew mom had arrived at the car, so I asked, "All right, mom, what ingredient did we forget?" She replied, "What type of salad are you making, Trisha?" I was talking all of this out loud for Jan's benefit, as she's not clairaudient, and we both shouted simultaneously, "We forgot the cans of fruit cocktail!" and laughed for several hours.Hearing voices can be helpful when looking for a lost item, making a recipe from memory, talking to the deceased to give messages to clients, warnings of danger, finding a parking place close to the front, and many other things.

It is not suggested that you publicly announce that you "hear voices." Unfortunately, many people have been put on heavy medication or locked away in an institution for such beliefs. However, those that know and love us understand that being clairaudient is okay, so we are safer with them. At a young age, I told Spirit that our agreement is: "My obedience with my gifts, and the world not locking me away THIS lifetime!"

LISTEN HERE

HOLD YOUR CAMERA OVER THE QR CODE. GET ACCESS TO MY MEDITATION THAT HELPS YOU ACTIVATE YOUR CLAIRAUDIENCE GIFT.

"When we Ask,
    Believe and are in
        Alignment, it's magical
            to Receive Abundance
                in all areas of life."

Trisha

CHAPTER FIVE

TRUST YOUR FEELINGS

When I'm facilitating workshops on the Clairs, the most hands are raised, acknowledging that they are clairsentients. Of all of the psychic gifts, being clairsentient is the most prevalent. Many of these clients have said that it's a curse instead of a blessing. They do not like feeling so emotional or being told they are over-sensitive. Understanding how this talent operates, making adjustments accordingly, shifting their belief from cursed to blessed can be a significant life change. It's a kind Universe. Keeping that in mind, you can flourish outside of your home.

Developing your Clairsentience (clear feelings)

Clairsentients receive guidance through their intuitive gut feelings and hunches. Much of this style comes from the stomach region, where the stomach flutters, relaxes, and clinches, tightens, feeling the sense of something. Clairsentients get messages through their hearts and love emotions as well. If a thought of doing something swells in your chest with warm feelings of joy, this is a directive from Spirit/Source/God/Angels. These effects are also signs of Clairsentience:

- Goosebumps or chills
- Temperature changes
- Cold hands/feet, flushed face
- Tingling, or a light breeze
- Sensing a presence or an energy
- Feeling a slight touch
- Tingling sensation or pressure at the top of head (crown)
- Pressure at the base of your skull
- Slight dizziness or vertigo as you connect/disconnect from channeling
- Smelling a scent without a physical source

Many people with clairsentience abilities find all feelings, emotions, noises overwhelming, even to anxiety attacks. You may be more comfortable or familiar with Empath (Empathic). It is a term more widely used. Many books are written about coping with overwhelming sensations. Creating a routine allows familiarity, comfort, and, therefore, less anxiety. Being aware of your surroundings is essential, focused, but not hypersensitive might make an anxiety attack. Maintaining balance in your life will help create a sense of well-being.

The Bubble Up method seems to assist the clairsentient clients the most. Keeping their energy inside the barrier and other people's energy outside the Bubble helps separate the energy, therefore, not "taking on" other's vibrations. In addition, creating the separation aids in feeling less overwhelmed.

Clairsentient Practice Exercise
Remember to use your protection method before starting the pendulum exercise:

Pendulum:
The pendulum is a powerful divination tool that dates back to ancient Egypt; like the Tarot, it is also helpful for accessing information from your higher self and should be used for questions with "YES" and "NO" answers.

Choosing a Pendulum:
- When held lightly in your dominant hand, it can be placed between your index finger and thumb or balanced between your index finger and middle finger (in the groove of the fingers toward the palm).
- The pendulum should start moving or spinning by itself (you are not making it move). If it doesn't move at all, pick another pendulum.

After finding a device with movement energy, it's ready for programming.

Programming a Pendulum:
Some books talk about clockwise and counter-clockwise directions representing YES and NO. I like to keep things simple. Up and Down movement is YES, as that's how your

head moves when you say the word yes. Left and Right movements represent NO because that is the direction your head moves when you say the word no.

- Programming your pendulum, you say: "Show me Yes (moving your head up & down)" Then, "Show me No (moving your head left & right)."
- After the programming is complete, your device is now moving automatically when you say yes and no; you need to teach it to CLEAR Say: "Show me Clear (it will start spinning in a circle, clearing the energy)."
- Now you are ready to ask questions. Keep the questions simple. Yes or No answers. Clear in between responses.

There are books with charts in them that have the alphabets, body organs, maps, etc. where more detailed answers can be asked and answered.

Channeling

The channeling process is similar to meditation. Meditation introspection allows one to gain inner clarity and wisdom. Channeling is the process of verbal communication expressing truth and understanding for others, facilitating specific answers to specific questions. During Mediumship, you are aware of your surroundings, although in an altered state, whereas during meditation, you are not. Having Clairsentience will amp up your sensitivities. Don't let this be alarming. Using your protection method will help you feel safe. Sometimes channeling is a phenomenon where an entity speaks through a living human being. This process is known as Trans Channeling.

This is not how my gift operates, but some famous Mediums work this way (Esther Hicks channels "Abraham").

During the channeling process, the vast consciousness is opened for the reception. That means that an entity may be an angel (ArchAngel Michael or Gabriel), an Ascended Master (Ramtha or Lazaris), or simply a wise and aware human being who has departed this Earth (Albert Einstein or Thomas Edison), to name a few. You receive Guides when you are born, and additional guides come in and out of your life as needed. An example, Quan Yin came into my life when I received my Reiki Master attunement. I've always admired her, what she represents, "Goddess of Mercy" - compassion, but from that point forward, I could see her (Clairvoyance) besides feeling her presents (Clairsentience).

Holding a Channel-Faced Crystal during the channeling process assists many clairsentients to feel more grounded, amplifying the energy-giving more clarity in receiving the information. A channeling crystal has a face with seven edges; the back of the channel face is usually a triangle.

Channeling or Mediumship exercise:
- Take slow, deep breaths through your nose exhale through your open mouth.
- Relax
- Breathing deeply, imagine a golden thread of energy coming from the stars, down through the top of your head.
- Continue to imagine this golden light flowing down each of the chakras (energy centers).
- Imagine the golden light moving down each leg, through the bottoms of your feet.
- As the golden light moves out of the feet, imagine it

continuing down through the ground, down to the center of the Earth.

- Imagine there is a giant Quartz crystal in the center of the Earth, now being filled with golden light.
- Breathe in through your nose, exhale through your open mouth.
- Through this process, you connect your energy with the Divine/Source/Angels.

Discomfort may be a physical effect of clairsentient enhancing their gifts. The more focused the exercise sometimes may result in feeling:

- Slight dizziness or vertigo as you connect/disconnect (tip: If you feel disoriented for an extended period after disconnecting. Be sure to ground more fully).
- Sweating, feeling a sudden urgency to go to the bathroom (tip: The stimulation of the endocrine, excretory and digestive systems due to increased vibration of energy running through the physical body, which creates rapid detoxification on the cellular level. Drinking pure water to flush out these systems is an effective way to clear the body).

Acupressure is known worldwide for targeting blocks in your energy system and clearing that point, thus enabling the energy to flow freely and allowing your body to heal itself. Emotions have an energetic charge and get stuck somewhere in your body. The belief that emotions cause disease is not a new one. The studies concerning stress are overpowering in their outcome. Stress causes physical problems. Emotional trauma causes physical problems. Being Clairsentient causes additional energy to be activated in your body, so clearing the body of energy blocks can allow tremendous success when channeling.

Clearing your consciousness for Channeling

In this exercise, you will be holding specific energy points to amp up the process of Channeling. "Third eye point" is located in the middle of the forehead and increases psychic vision. The "Inner Eye Points" are where every acupressure meridian enters the brain. Finally, the "Under Eye points" address fear, so clearing this area will allow confidence with your spiritual gifts.

- Hold the points with a light touch.
- Your thumb and fourth (ring) finger hold the inner eye points.
- Your Pinky finger rests on either of the under eye points.
- Your forefinger and middle finger rest at the corners of the third eye- imagine that you are slightly stretching the third eye open (You really are).

Psychometry or psychoscopy is the ability to obtain information about a person or object, usually by touch. For example, the lounge magicians use this technique to know who an item belongs to in the audience. Several people from the audience place a personal item on a tray. The tray is then carried forward to the magician. One by one, the things are handled and given to the correct member of the audience.

When purchasing "used" items, it's best to clear the item's energy so that the prior owner's energy does not stay with the thing. Antiques hold many lifetimes of owners' energies on them.

(Clearing/smudging process was discussed in Chapter 3).

Channeling is similar to playing piano: almost anyone who applies himself can probably learn to do it, at least a little, and even a casual study of it can be enriching. However, learning to do it well requires a lot of energy and commitment, and obviously, it comes more easily to some people than to others. Furthering our skills in this lifetime, whatever they are, can lead to being born with more "talent" in those areas in future lifetimes.

CHAPTER SIX

BELIEVE WHAT YOU SEE

Developing Clairvoyance (clear sight)

As I mentioned before, Clairvoyance is my most vital gift. So when asked, "When did you realize you were psychic?" my response is quite simple, "I've always been this way. I'm not unique because I never realized everyone couldn't see or hear dead people."

Seeing a dearly departed loved one, angels, ascended masters, teachers, scientists, and explorers are among the fantastic experiences of receiving messages from their wisdom while channeling. When the movie "Sixth Sense" came out, I was excited to be able to reference it when explaining my talents. I'm grateful that I'm not shown all of the gore of the dead like in the movie. A psychic friend and editor, DeWitt Lobrano, refers to these entities as DPs (Dead People). My psychic gift comes with humor, as does his I love joking and laughing with the departed people and my clients. Grief is a heavy vibration. It can make the energy in the room dense, causing it more difficult to Channel Laughter raises the frequency. As the clients', the room's, and the medium's vibration rise, the connection to the DPs are more vital, which assists in the communication process. The dimension where the others reside is a higher frequency than we are in our dimension. Those of you who have attended my show "Hello Again from the Other Side," where I Channel giving the audience members messages, know that I make fun of your dearly departed loved ones.

Some of the ways you may recognize that you are clairvoyant:

- Pressure or tingling between your physical eyes or third eye, which aligns with your eyebrows, between the physical eyes, in the middle of your forehead.
- You see symbols, colors, words, energies, pictures, or streaming video through your third eye or your mind's eye.
- You see orbs or flashes of white or colored lights with your physical eyes (Auras).

If you answered YES to any or all of these occurrences, intentionally opening the third eye may assist you to "see" more clearly.

Clairvoyance Practice Exercise Opening the Third Eye:

<u>Remember</u> to use your protection method before starting the exercise.

Sit comfortably (If you lie down, you may fall asleep).

- Begin this exercise by focusing on your breath.
- Place your hand on your stomach. Breathe deeply, filling your abdomen and lungs thoroughly, and feel your hand move outward.
- Then with an open mouth, exhale slowly from your lungs to your abdomen, feeling your hand move back toward your body.
- Continue to breathe in this manner until you reach a state of relaxation. Concentrate on your breath. Noises around you do not matter.
- Close your eyes Using your index finger, touch the spot just above the area between your physical eyes on your forehead. Gently slide your finger in an upward direction as if prying the eyelid of your third eye open.
- Focus on the screen behind your closed eyes. Your third eye will begin to open - observe colors. Seeing color is not your imagination. Note the color. When you do, stop to rest.
- Slowly return to your body by focusing on your breath.
- Breathe deeply, filling your abdomen and lungs thoroughly, then exhale slowly from your lungs to your abdomen. Consciously move your hands, feet, legs, and arms and slowly open your eyes. Once alert, journal your experience.

Begin the breathing process again.

- Watch the screen behind your closed eyes. Observe shapes. After seeing colors, you may see shapes. When you see a shape observe it lightly, stop to rest.

- Slowly return to your body by focusing on your breath.
- Breathe deeply, filling your abdomen and lungs thoroughly, then exhale slowly from your lungs to your abdomen. Consciously move your hands, feet, legs, and arms and slowly open your eyes. Once alert, journal your experience.

Begin the breathing process again.

- Watch the screen behind your closed eyes. Observe images. If an image appears, imagine that you are moving closer to examine it. Notice any details, however obscure, including movement. You are an observer, not a participant. Stop to rest.
- Return to your body by focusing on your breath. Breathe deeply, filling your abdomen and lungs thoroughly, then exhale slowly from your lungs to your abdomen. Consciously move your hands, feet, legs, and arms and slowly open your eyes. Once alert, journal your experience.

When you have completed each step separately, you may then do the exercise observing colors, shapes, and objects in one session. When you have been successful with this process of seeing all, there is a technique below teaching you a quicker method of activating your third eye.

Some people have told me that they get a headache doing this technique. It is temporary. When we are young, we are profoundly clairvoyant. As society tells us that it's not "normal" behavior, or we are frightened by a message from another realm, we learn to shut down/off our gifts to "fit in." Using a muscle (opening your closed third eye) can be uncomfortable at first. It gets easier. It becomes natural again and free of discomfort.

Exercises to develop ease into clairvoyant activity:

Once you get the above process down, you can create a simple method to move right into clairvoyant activity - Using a hypnosis word: Trigger.

Set the trigger using the following method. Then when you want to focus on your clairvoyant sight, you will just use the trigger process:
Sit comfortably.

- Relax your body, Shake off any stress being held in your body Breathe in deeply, filling your abdomen and lungs fully, then exhale slowly from your lungs to your abdomen with an open mouth, until you reach a state of relaxation Concentrate on your breath Noises around you do not matter.
- Focus your awareness on your heart center. Breathe in three cleansing breaths through your heart, slowing your mind and body to a peaceful state of being.
- Decide what your physical trigger will be. For example, "Each time I tap my third eye (middle of the forehead above your physical eyes), I will instantly be in an open, receptive state."
- Say this to yourself about ten (10) times as you go through the motions. Each time you tap your third eye

area on your forehead, notice how relaxed you feel. Be sure to pay attention to the physical sensations you are experiencing as you program this process.

- Once you have completed the programming of your subconscious command, you have created a Trigger Release.

Now when you want to have a clairvoyant experience, you will breathe deeply, get relaxed, tap your third eye, become more relaxed, and the visions will now appear.

The behavior needs to be repeated consistently for 21 days to create a habit. After that, you will be able to use your trigger and drop into the clairvoyant process through practice. I recommend journaling, as we tend to forget what we "saw" during a session. Do your best not to question (logical mind) what you are seeing. You may receive a message from a friend or family member. Share the information with them without being attached to their response.

It may not mean anything to them when the message is delivered, yet later appear with an understanding. It is not about being right or wrong. No judgment should be made working with your gift.

Another result of being clairvoyant can show up by having prophetic visions and dreams. Sometimes, dreams include all of your senses creating an experience versus viewing it as a movie. There are times when you will be given a warning of something that might happen to you or someone you know in a dream; this is known as a prophetic dream or vision. When we dream, it can be simply your subconscious working out the day's events while you sleep. Maybe you disagreed with someone, perhaps you watched a news broadcast or a movie before going to bed, and you are reliving the experience in your dream, possibly trying to create a different outcome. Dreams are a series of pictures, images, ideas in a visual form and are primarily symbols to represent meaning. There are many books written for Dream Interpretation. Journal your dream as soon as you wake up. Grab your book to interpret your dream and write what you think it means. Writing it down (the symbols) and the meaning aid you in getting answers and strengthen the clairvoyant gift.

One day, when my son was only a few months old, my mother in-law wanted to take him to visit her family (I was not invited). As she pleaded with me, I kept telling her that I had a "bad feeling." She continued to remind me that she raised three boys and would be fine with her grandson.
Finally, as I passed her the baby, I received a flash -a snapshot- of my son flying out of the windshield, dying in an auto accident. I screamed, grabbed my son, sobbing, and told her about my vision. She thought I was nuts. This argument took place over 20-30 minutes. Finally, when she arrived home, she told me that there was no car accident. I know, to this day, that the delay of the argument and not allowing her to take my son saved his life. Sometimes we don't have proof that an event would have occurred, but in my soul, I know.

Knowingness Cards ™

Knowingness Cards are a unique and fun way to help you develop your psychic gifts. The cards are designed to help you connect with your intuition, increase your awareness and strengthen your communication outside of normal sensory capability, as in telepathy and clairvoyance. Each card has a different symbol, which can help you to focus your thoughts and open up your intuition. The cards are a great way to test your ESP, as they can help you to better understand your extrasensory perception.

The Knowingness Cards are a deck of twenty-five cards, five of each symbol. The five symbols are a heart, a halo, an arrow, stars, and angel wings. At a young age I played with tools similar to these cards.

As a test for ESP, the experimenter picks up a card in a shuffled pack, observes the symbol, and records the answer of the tested person, who would guess which of the five designs was on the card. The experimenter continues until all the cards in the pack are tested. Grab your deck of Knowingness cards at **KnowingnessCards.com**.

How to test your ESP with Knowingness Cards:
- Use a sheet of paper and write down the numbers 1-25.
- Shuffle the cards.
- Place the first card, picture down, in front of you.
- Concentrate on the card.
- Now write down the symbol's shape on your sheet of paper.
- Take the next card, place it face down on top of the prior card.
- Concentrate on the card.
- Write the image on the piece of paper.
- Continue this method until all of the card images have been written on the piece of paper.
- Now you turn over the pile of 25 cards.
- One by one, check the card against the answer on your piece of paper.

Doing this process of "viewing" the Knowingness cards, strengthens the mind-eye connection, increasing the clairvoyance ability.

Tarot and Oracle Cards

Many people with Clairvoyance find the Tarot or oracles to aid them with their "visions." As with choosing a crystal or pendulum, picking a deck of cards to use is a personal choice.

Being very left-brained, my logical brian thought, I had to memorize the means of the cards and use that knowledge to do a reading. Although I took Tarot classes, it became my experience that the cards were used to flash images, or ideas, from one thought to the next, or to receive an answer to a specific question with an image from the card. I've been using the Thoth deck for over 25 years. I have over 30 other decks that have "called out to me." Still, the Thoth remains my trusted, comfortable friend.

After choosing a deck, you need to adjust the frequency to your energy field. Many intuitives prefer not to let another person touch their deck because it is tuned for them.

- Open the package of cards.
- Touch each card, looking at the picture, create a new pile from the cards you have touched.
- Pick up the viewed, touched cards.
- Fan them out.
- Hold them in a fanned pattern with your right hand.
- Place the deck over your heart.
- Breathe deeply, in through the nose, exhale through your opened mouth.
- Visualize a good memory in your life. Love.
- Thank the cards for supporting you and being a good assistance to your clairvoyance gift.

Now you are ready to use the divination tool. You may use the cards for your introspection or give a reading to someone else. Always show your deck care reverence.

Many books, even one that comes with your deck, show

different layouts. Celtic Cross is used most frequently. I'm not a conventional Medium, so I place three cards down which tell my Guides, "Ready, Set, Go!". Then as I start receiving information, relaying it to my client, I will put another card on top of another as a "signifier," giving me more details on the card it covered (another card still peeking out from under it).

A great way to begin reading cards is by picking three cards to start your day—Past, Present, and Future. Then, write what you think the cards mean for you for that day in a journal. Next, please write in your journal what they represented, comparing the notes from earlier in the day. Doing this activity for 21-30 consecutive days gives you the confidence to read for other people.

Seeing Auras

A young lady told me that she was seeing flashing lights. She was concerned that she had developed an eye problem. So she went to see an optometrist who specializes in mind-eye connection. Upon further examination, the doctor told her that there was no eye injury or illness in the eyes that she is clairvoyant. This young woman is an artist and uses her Clairvoyance to create unique works of art. As she has developed her talents more, the eyes, or signal from the eyes, changed the method of communication or frequency. So now, the flashing lights were a signal from the brain that she was ready to create an image or piece of art.

Some cameras capture the frequency around you. For example, you place your hand on a metallic plate (conductor). The signal is then transferred through a computer's software, indicating the vibration in the areas around the body image.

The colors and size of the aura can be transmitted to sensor plates and captured in the photograph.

TEST YOUR ESP

HOLD YOUR CAMERA OVER THE QR CODE. TEST YOUR ESP WITH YOUR OWN DECK OF KNOWINGNESS CARDS.

CHAPTER SEVEN

UNDERSTANDING

Most of you reading this book have already had years of practice with your gifts. You have created coping skills to filter when or how you use these talents. We all have access to all four ways of communication. Usually, we have one primary way of receiving guidance and one secondary way of communication. You can become proficient at receiving messages in all four ways with practice. At the beginning of training, most people concentrate upon their natural means of communication.

There are two core functions to communicate with Spirit.
1) to promote a greater sense of God-self and
2) realization of your purpose in life.

Native American Story: An elder Cherokee chief took his grandchildren into the forest, sat them down, and said: "A fight is going on inside me. This is a terrible fight, and it is a fight between two wolves. One wolf is the wolf of fear, anger, arrogance, and greed. The other is the wolf of courage, kindness, humility, and love."

The children were very quiet and listened to their grandfather with both ears. He then said, "This same fight between the wolves that is going on inside of me is going on inside of you and every person."

The children thought about this for a minute, and then one child asked the chief, "Grandfather, which wolf will win the fight?"

He said quietly, "The one you feed!"

Feed your soul. Feed your gifts, talents, and Clairs. Through the techniques given here, you will gain confidence and peace of mind knowing that you, too, are psychic. Yes, Everyone is!

CHAPTER EIGHT

GRATITUDE MANIFESTATION JOURNAL

THE WAY TO ACCELERATE YOUR DESIRES INTO REALITY

As you strengthen your psychic abilities you will understand that a large part of manifesting your desires and goals in life is to have an attitude of gratitude. When you are truly grateful and give heartfelt thanks for everything you already have in your life, you will start to attract more things to be thankful for.

I have always used a daily gratitude journal, and from personal experience this supercharges the manifestation of your desires into your reality. To have an attitude of gratitude is like pressing the accelerator button on your wishes!

Using my signature Gratitude Manifestation Journal will be your secret, unfair advantage to intuitively bring your cognitions into your present reality and reach your goals faster.

Simply put, when this journal becomes part of your daily life, you will create more with less overwhelm and stress.

How to Use Your Journal Effectively

Each day uses two pages. The first page is where you give thanks for the day you have just experienced; the second page is for the following day, where you include all the things you want to attract that day.

The key here is to keep everything you write in your journal in the present tense. Even the things you want to attract during the following day need to be written in present tense.. For example, start each sentence with - I am so happy and grateful now that I am so thankful. Then, as you write your first day about what you have just experienced in the present tense, write the second page in the same way, as if it has already happened.

I would recommend starting with more minor things you would like to attract into the following day. As you see these things begin to appear in your life "as if by magic," your belief system will strengthen, and you will be able to build on your conscious creation and manifestation of the ideal things you desire in life.

Another great benefit of completing a gratitude journal is that you regularly put yourself in a good feeling place. When you are in a good feeling place, more things to feel good about will show up in your life.

On a final note, when you use this method, you will also need to stay open and ready to continue your days in a positive state filled with gratitude. Knowing all is well, you are right where you should be in life, even if it doesn't seem that way in the beginning is an attitude of gratitude.

Trust me, as the magic of your psychic gifts and the universal power of the Law of Attraction unfolds, you will be blessed at what shows up in your life!

To learn my unique, yet simple process to effectively use my signature gratitude manifestation journal, go watch the quick tutorial I created for you now by scanning the QR Code below. This journal is designed to help you eliminate uncertainty, stop procrastination, clarify your thoughts, fine tune your desires and manifest more.

Don't put off watching the tutorial. Life is easier and more fun when the messages are clear. Go watch now.

Support on Your Journey

My team and I use these exact same journals every day of the week. They are my passion. So, if you have any questions please don't hesitate to reach out to us via email.

I am beyond confident that in just 14 days from now you will feel the difference in the four psychic senses by using this journal properly.

You are officially on your journey and you too are psychic, everyone is. Welcome!

WATCH HERE

HOLD YOUR CAMERA OVER THE QR CODE. GET ACCESS TO MY INSTRUCTIONS.

Today I am

_____

_____

_____

_____

_____

_____

_____

_____

_____

_____

_____

_____

I AM HAVING THE
EXACT EXPERIENCE
NEEDED FOR MY
AWAKENING

Tomorrow I get to

Today I am

Nothing ever
goes away
until it teaches us
what we need
to know.

Tomorrow I get to

Today I am

You know who's gonna give you
everything? _yourself._

Tomorrow I get to

Today I am

_____

_____

_____

_____

_____

_____

_____

_____

_____

_____

_____

Everything Heals.

Your body heals.
Your heart heals.
Your mind heals.
Your happiness is going to come back.
Bad times don't last.

Tomorrow I get to

Today I am

I am an unlimited being
in an unlimited universe

Tomorrow I get to

Today I am

_____

_____

_____

_____

_____

_____

_____

_____

_____

_____

_____

_____

_____

_____

Notice the
beautiful moments

_____

_____

_____

Tomorrow I get to

Today I am

Never suppress a generous thought

Tomorrow I get to

Today I am

_____

_____

_____

_____

_____

_____

_____

_____

_____

_____

_____

_____

_____

I am strong   _____

_____

Tomorrow I get to

Today I am

I am decisive

Tomorrow I get to

Today I am

I am grateful

Tomorrow I get to

Today I am

I am abundant

Tomorrow I get to

Today I am

Everything is
figureoutable

Tomorrow I get to

Today I am

_____

_____

_____

_____

_____

_____

_____

_____

_____

_____

_____

_____

_____

_____

_____

_____

CREATE GOOD KARMA

Tomorrow I get to

Today I am

I know a beautiful soul
when I feel one.

Tomorrow I get to

Today I am

_____

_____

_____

_____

_____

_____

_____

_____

_____

_____

_____

_____

_____

_____

_____

Everything you want is coming.
Relax and let the universe pick the timing
and the way. You just need to trust that
what you want is coming and watch how
fast it comes.

Tomorrow I get to

Today I am

_Never underestimate the power
of speaking with love_

Tomorrow I get to

Today I am

I am physically, mentally and
emotionally ready to enter a new phase of
my life. I'm ready to grow and get better.

Tomorrow I get to

Today I am

your soul
is on the perfect journey

Tomorrow I get to

Today I am

turn off
tune in

Tomorrow I get to

Today I am

_____

_____

_____

_____

_____

_____

_____

_____

_____

_____

_____

_____

_____

_____

you are entirely up to you

Tomorrow I get to

Today I am

I release what's
holding me back and
blocking me

Tomorrow I get to

Today I am

_____

_____

_____

_____

_____

_____

_____

_____

_____

_____

_____

_____

_____

_____

and you've only just begun

Tomorrow I get to

Today I am

_____

_____

_____

_____

_____

_____

_____

_____

_____

_____

_____

_____

_____

_____

_____

Choose Purpose over Perfect

Tomorrow I get to

Today I am

_____
_____
_____
_____
_____
_____
_____
_____
_____
_____
_____

Law of attraction:

1. Create a clear vision
2. Connect with the universe
3. Feel grateful for everything
4. Surrender the outcome
5. Trust in divine timing

Tomorrow I get to

Today I am

I choose calm over anxiety

Tomorrow I get to

Today I am

THE SUN SEES YOUR BODY,
THE MOON SEES YOUR SOUL.

Tomorrow I get to

Today I am

_____
_____
_____
_____
_____
_____
_____
_____
_____
_____
_____
_____

Today I release:

- toxic thoughts and emotions

- unhealthy environments

- unfruitful relationships

- thoughts of revenge and unforgiveness

- negative words I've thought

- negative words I've spoken

Tomorrow I get to

Today I am

remember when you wanted
what you currently have?

Tomorrow I get to

Today I am

Owning your story

is the bravest thing you can do

Tomorrow I get to

Today I am

_____
_____
_____
_____
_____
_____
_____
_____
_____
_____
_____
_____
_____
_____
_____

How we walk with the broken
speaks louder than how we walk
with the Great

Tomorrow I get to

Today I am

Don't give up before
the miracle happens

Tomorrow I get to

Today I am

i decide my vibe

Tomorrow I get to

Today I am

SHOW UP,
BE BRAVE,
BE KIND,
REST,
AND,
TRY AGAIN

Tomorrow I get to

Today I am

COMMIT
TO THE
MOMENT

Tomorrow I get to

Today I am

You are made of
Stardust, Wishes
and Magical Things

Tomorrow I get to

Today I am

_____

Time heals nothing

unless you move along with it

Tomorrow I get to

Today I am

_____

_____

_____

_____

_____

_____

_____

_____

_____

_____

Authenticity

...is not something we have or don't have.
It's a practice -
a conscious choice of how we want to live.
Authenticity is a collection of choices
that we have to make every day.
The choice to let ourselves be seen.

Tomorrow I get to

look within

TRISHA DOLAN

Today I am

_____

_____

_____

_____

_____

_____

_____

_____

_____

_____

_____

WHAT IS MEANT FOR YOU, WON'T PASS YOU BY

Tomorrow I get to

Today I am

If speaking kindly
to plants helps them grow -
Imagine what speaking kindly
to humans can do.

Tomorrow I get to

Today I am

I can't wait to see how this
unfolds...

Tomorrow I get to

Today I am

I am whole

Tomorrow I get to

Today I am

when you love yourself,
you glow from the inside

Tomorrow I get to

Today I am

I AM HOPEFUL

Tomorrow I get to

Today I am

I AM LIGHT

Tomorrow I get to

Today I am

I am brave

Tomorrow I get to

Today I am

BE KIND

Tomorrow I get to

Today I am

She's got that
sophisticated, street
smart, spiritual,
soulful, savage thing
about her

Tomorrow I get to

Today I am

THE EMPATH IN ME,
HONORS
THE AUTHENTIC
IN YOU

Tomorrow I get to

Today I am

_____

_____

_____

_____

_____

_____

_____

_____

_____

_____

_____

Go Inward.

That's the real work.

The solutions are not outside of us.

Get to know who you really are because as you

search for the hero within, you inevitably

become one.

Tomorrow I get to

Today I am

You receive the same energy as
you put out. Be even more
supportive, grateful and kind.
Watch how things change.

Tomorrow I get to

Today I am

Lie down for 10 mins and just breathe.
Unplug from the chaos of life long enough
to connect with whatever calms you.

Tomorrow I get to

Today I am

You receive the same energy as
you put out. Be even more
supportive, grateful and kind.
Watch how things change.

Tomorrow I get to

Today I am

Protect your peace.
Get rid of toxicity.
Cleanse your space.
Cultivate love.

Tomorrow I get to

Today I am

_____

What if we recharged ourselves
as often as we did our phones?

Tomorrow I get to

Today I am

_____

_____

_____

_____

_____

_____

_____

_____

_____

_____

ALMOST EVERYTHING _____

WILL WORK AGAIN _____

IF YOU UNPLUG IT. _____

INCLUDING YOU. _____

_____

192   TRISHA DOLAN

Tomorrow I get to

Today I am

_____

_____

_____

_____

_____

_____

_____

_____

_____

IN EVERY MOMENT
OF THE DAY,
I RADIATE CALMNESS AND
TRANQUILITY.
I AM STILL WITHIN MYSELF

Tomorrow I get to

Today I am

I am evolving
&
it's so damn beautiful

Tomorrow I get to

Today I am

It's not selfish to love yourself,
take care of yourself and to make
your happiness a priority.

Tomorrow I get to

Today I am

_____

_____

_____

_____

_____

_____

_____

_____

_____

_____

_____

_____

_____

_____

I am attracting unconditional
love, abundance,
high vibrational experiences,
and sacred connections.

Tomorrow I get to

Today I am

I give up freely what is no
longer serving me.
I release it to create space for
what inspires me

Tomorrow I get to

Today I am

Consider becoming the type of energy that no matter where you go, or where you are, you add value to the spaces and lives around you.

Tomorrow I get to

Today I am

a few nice words can help someone
more than you think

Tomorrow I get to

Today I am

People always say they
wish life came with
instructions.
It does - *emotions.*

Tomorrow I get to

Acknowledgments

I WANT TO SEND GRATITUDE for this book to so many enlightened spiritual beings that are having a human experience. First and foremost to the many Real World Angel Journey Members who contributed their personal experiences and support during the development of this book. Without their insight and knowingness, this creation in its final manifestation would not have been possible.

To my family, for standing by me both in the early years and later during the stresses and pressures of travel and growing

demands on my time.

My deepest heartfelt gratitude also to the following notable people who helped make it possible for a more significant segment of the public to receive the guidance and methods that have been my life's work:

Your love, friendship, encouragement, and support have been a true blessing to My Best Friend (you know who you are). Thank you for always being a special person in my life.

To DeWitt Lobrano, thank you for your help outlining, editing, guiding me through the journey of getting the ideas out of my head and into print has indeed been a gift.

Your psychic insight and experiencing my passion gave me a different view to embrace my life's work.

To Jasper Dayton, major gratitude for pushing me out of my comfort zone and assisting me to create a way to give my calling a voice. Your ability to transform my thoughts into reality is a marvel. In addition, the mentorship in business processes and technology has been instrumental in
completing this book and in many ways of reaching the masses.

To Heidi Baker, my heart is full of gratitude for creating a way to join our International Sisters, a platform for public speaking and Time Talks' life-changing experience.

To Linet Andrea, thank you for being my tour guide in France, your encouragement to live my dreams of world travel, and your friendship.

To Marianne Simpson, Jennifer Meyer, Juaniece Bair, and Katharina Kaesbach, for traveling to Sedona, allowing me to be your spiritual guide in a sacred place retreat style. The bond we created will be forever in my heart. Thank you for the magical experience.

Also, a special thanks to the following You Too Are Psychic Students both for their contributions, hard work, and sincere dedication to You Too Are Psychic and the Real World Angel Method to show others how to be their teachers.

About the Author

TRISHA DOLAN started her spiritual journey over 60 years ago. Her mom told her that she was an easy child because she would put me in my playpen, and she would chatter away, entertaining and talking to herself. As Trisha got older, she continued to speak to her "imaginary" friends (what her mother called them). As Trisha's vocabulary became more proficient, she would ask her mother about the people she saw in the room, not truly understanding that she saw, heard, and talked to people who had passed away, people from other realms. Trisha's mom always thought that she was a bit different, but she didn't discount her abilities or encourage them. They just didn't discuss Trisha's unusual talents of seeing, feeling, and hearing things that her mother nor many people around her understood. Trisha has been a professional Psychic Medium Angel Therapy Practitioner for over three decades, and she serves thousands of clients globally. She is certified in Tarot and speaks on stages with the famous signature "Hello Again" LIVE in-person events. You can find Trisha online at RealWorldAngel.com.

RealWORLDAngel.COM

HOLD YOUR SMART PHONE'S CAMERA OVER THE QR CODE. CHOOSE YOUR JOURNEY.

JOIN THE JOURNEY

NOW THAT YOU 'VE HEARD my story and have a new understanding of how to unlock, expand and strengthen your psychic gifts, it's time for you to chart your path. Let's keep the connection going. Join me and other enlightened souls who say yes to the art of higher awareness and connection to Spirit every day. Scan this code for more content to help you choose your journey.

Visit us online to access these free resources:

 Get connected with my community

Join my Free community, Real World Angel on Facebook and engage with enlightened souls that say yes to connecting with spirit.

 Connect with a community of people that are awakening to the art of connections and enlightenment. **facebook.com/groups/realworldangel**

 CALCULATE your sensitivities to Mercury Retrograde

How does Mercury Retrograde affect you? Take this quick calculation and find out. If you have experienced any of these events during the last Mercury Retrograde period, mark your score for each of the different events.

 Find out how sensitive you are to Mercury Retrograde. **www.RealWorldAngel.com/sensitivities**

 DISCOVER Angel Abundance Currency™

Accelerate your abundance with this proven breakthrough method to increase financial prosperity:

 Join now and receive FREE Moon Cycle reminders that increase your prosperity. **AngelAbundanceCurrency.com**

 APPLY to be a member of my Medium MASTERMIND Mentorship

The MASTERMIND Mentorship program is an exclusive community of industry professionals, healers and thought leaders–exclusive to those who qualify and meet specific criteria.

 Apply to be our next member **www.RealWorldAngel.com/application**

Made in the USA
Columbia, SC
06 August 2022

64421362R00122